First Published in Great Britain by
Powerfresh Limited
3 Gray Street
Northampton
England
NN1 3QQ

Telephone 0604 30996 Country Code 44
Facsimile 0604 21013

IT'S A BOY
ISBN 1 874125 28 7

Printed in Britain by Avalon Print Ltd., Northampton.

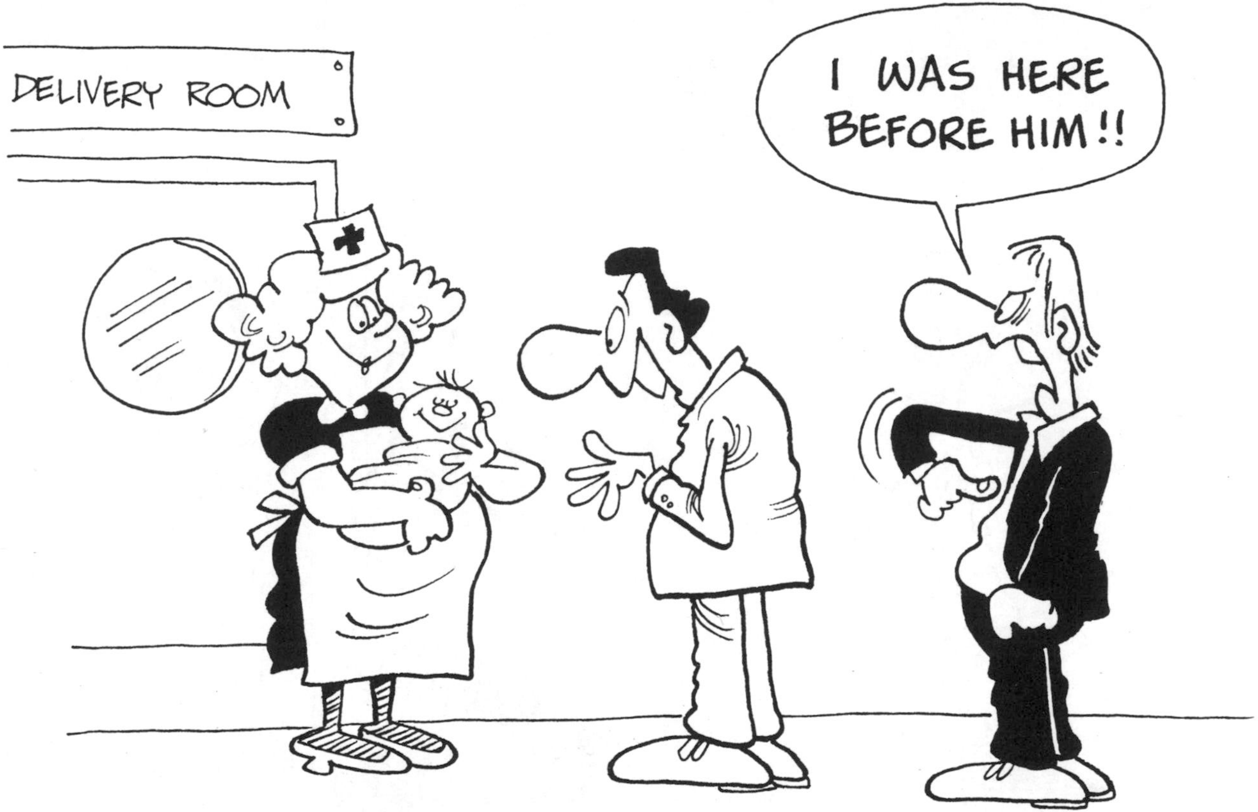
DELIVERY ROOM
I WAS HERE BEFORE HIM!!

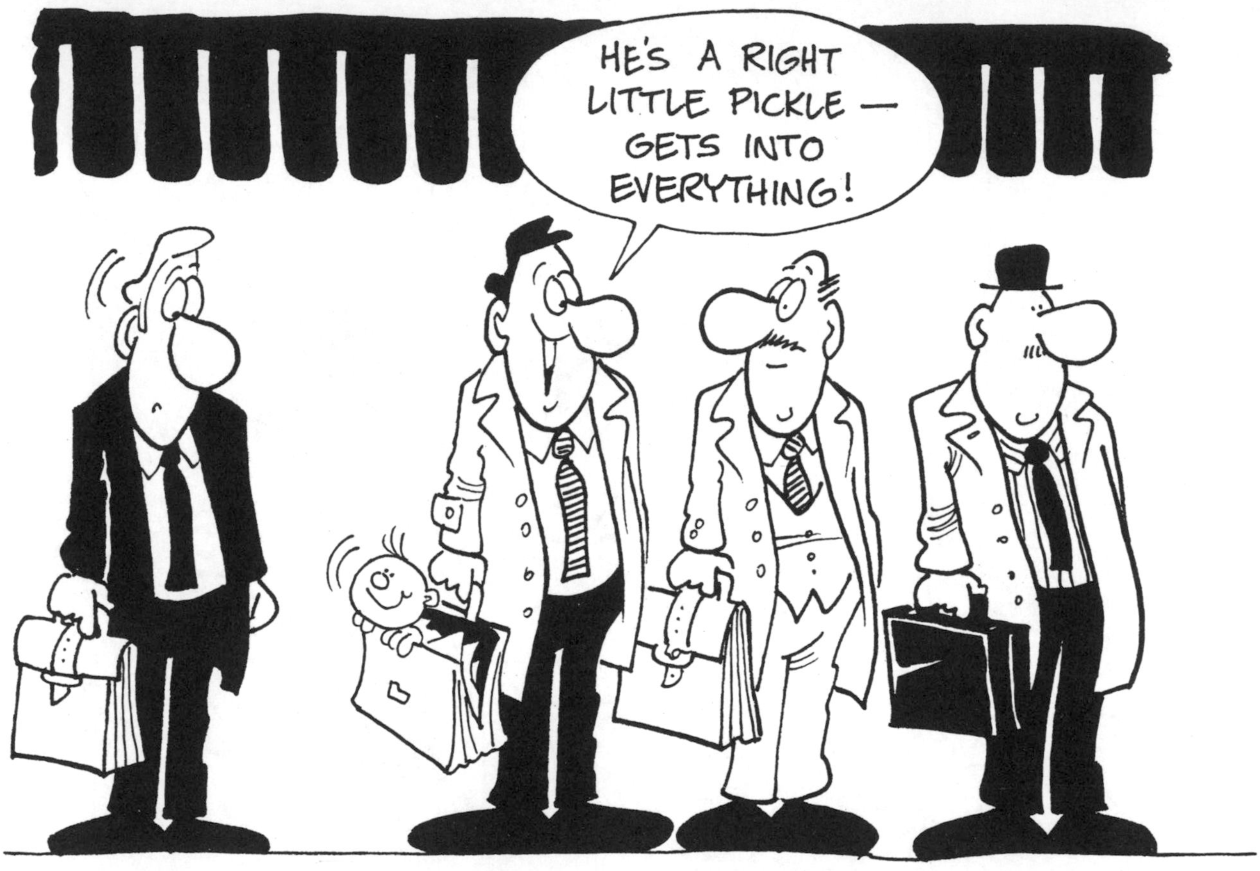
HE'S A RIGHT LITTLE PICKLE — GETS INTO EVERYTHING!

First Published in Great Britain by
Powerfresh Limited
3 Gray Street
Northampton
England
NN1 3QQ

Telephone 0604 30996 Country Code 44
Facsimile 0604 21013

IT'S A BOY
ISBN 1 874125 28 7

Printed in Britain by Avalon Print Ltd., Northampton.